In this Webb image a young cluster of stars lights up nearby gas and dust in the Orion Nebula.

UNLOCKING THE UNIVERSE

SUZANNE SLADE

UNLOCKING THE UNIVERSE

The Cosmic Discoveries of the Webb Space Telescope

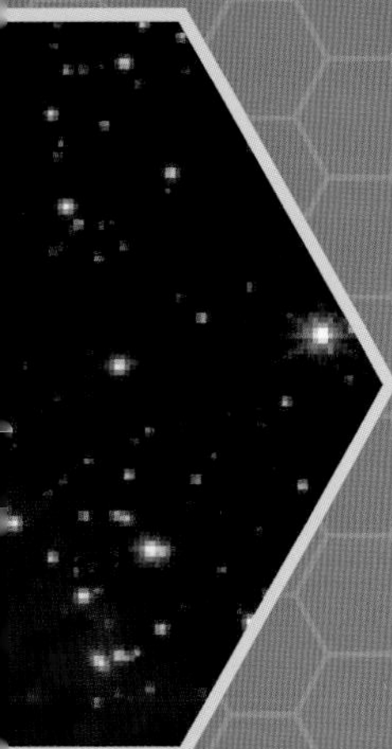

Charlesbridge

Space is mesmerizing and mysterious. We've learned a lot about our universe, but there are still so many secrets yet to be revealed.

Since the beginning of time, humans have been curious about the cosmos. But how can we explore the vastness of space from our small planet?

Thanks to human ingenuity, we've discovered a great deal from space missions, satellites, and telescopes. Sending telescopes into space is especially helpful. A space telescope operates above our atmosphere, which allows it to collect more and different kinds of light than telescopes on Earth. That light can be used to create incredible space images that give us a more complete view of the universe.

While orbiting the Sun from 2003 to 2020, the Spitzer Space Telescope used infrared light to study comets, galaxies, exoplanets (planets outside our solar system), and more. It created this gorgeous image of a nebula, a cloud of gas and dust in space. People say the bright spots near the top look like the eyes and nose of a dragon.

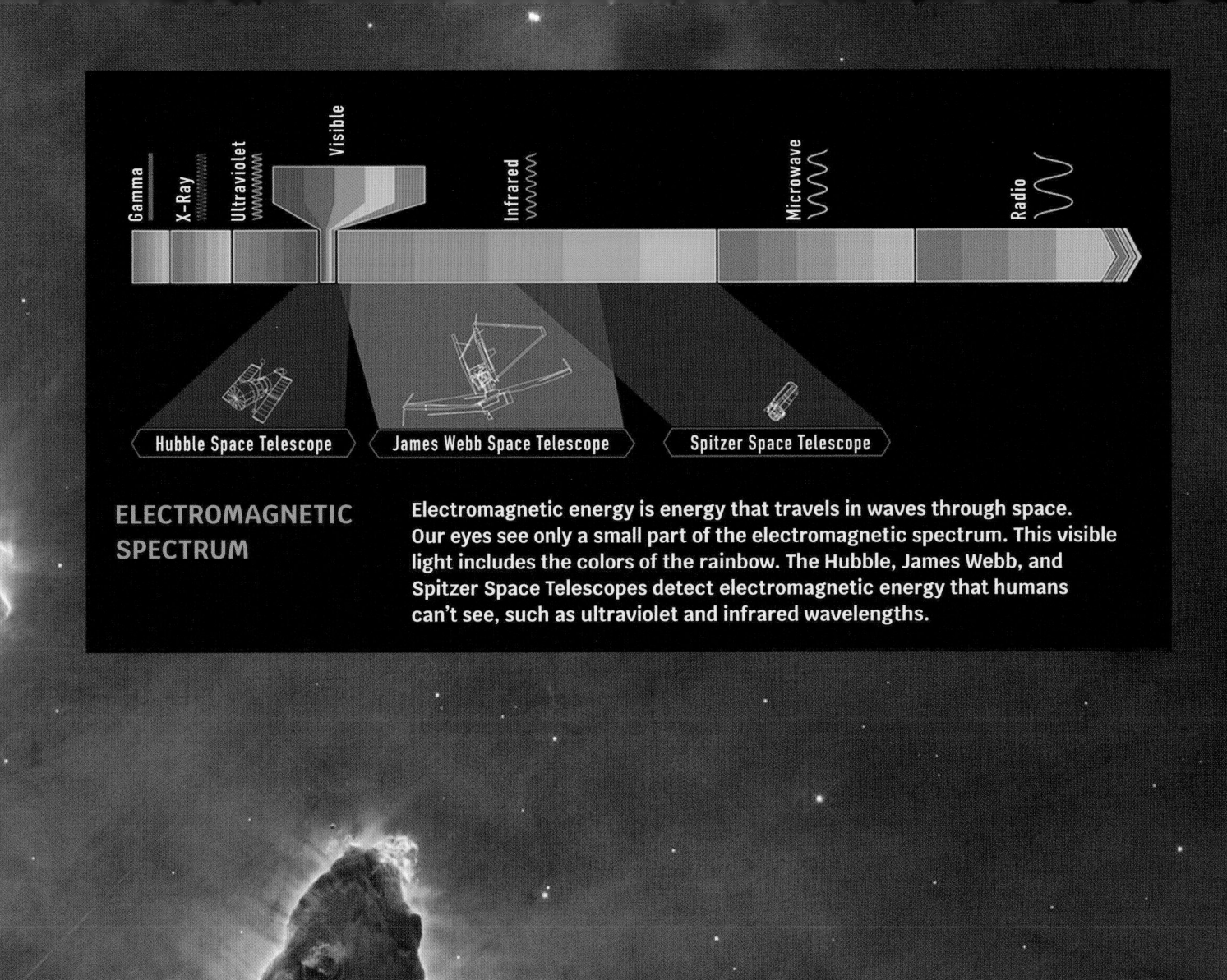

Gamma · X-Ray · Ultraviolet · Visible · Infrared · Microwave · Radio

Hubble Space Telescope · James Webb Space Telescope · Spitzer Space Telescope

ELECTROMAGNETIC SPECTRUM

Electromagnetic energy is energy that travels in waves through space. Our eyes see only a small part of the electromagnetic spectrum. This visible light includes the colors of the rainbow. The Hubble, James Webb, and Spitzer Space Telescopes detect electromagnetic energy that humans can't see, such as ultraviolet and infrared wavelengths.

Launched in 1990, the powerful Hubble Space Telescope views the universe mainly in visible and ultraviolet light, with some infrared light capability. It created this image of the Pillars of Creation, three towers of gas and dust in the Eagle Nebula. The hardworking Hubble is still circling Earth, creating amazing images.

So scientists dreamed up an advanced telescope—one that would soar through space and get a closer look. And they dreamed big!

In 1989, top astronomers and scientists gathered to discuss a revolutionary telescope that would orbit the Sun and peer farther into space than any previous telescope. Its huge primary mirror would collect large amounts of infrared light to create clearer, more detailed images than ever before. Infrared light is given off by every object in the universe and can travel through dust that blocks visible light.

The **Orion Nebula** is a massive cosmic cloud that contains more than one thousand young stars. NASA's Spitzer and Hubble Space Telescopes collected the infrared and visible light used to create this composite image of the nebula.

This colorful image of the Pinwheel Galaxy was created with data from different kinds of light (infrared, visible, ultraviolet, and X-ray) gathered by four NASA space telescopes: Spitzer, Hubble, GALEX, and the Chandra X-ray Observatory.

With this new telescope, astronomers planned to study our solar system, create images of distant galaxies, determine if other planets could support life, and even peer back in time to when the first stars formed.

After years of planning, scientists completed their innovative telescope design, which they named the Next Generation Space Telescope (NGST).

One of their goals was to look back in time. More than 13 billion years ago, the first stars formed and started giving off light. Some of that light has been traveling through space ever since. Scientists wanted to use the NGST to collect the light and create images of those newborn stars.

Another goal was to search for Earth-like exoplanets that might host life. The NGST would look for signs of water, carbon dioxide, and methane, which could indicate the possibility of life.

In 1996 the NGST team pitched the idea for their grand telescope to NASA. After thoroughly evaluating the design, NASA announced the project was a go.

Although light travels at a swift 300,000 kilometers (186,000 miles) per second, space is so gigantic that it can take many years for light from a distant star to reach our planet. Light from the Andromeda Galaxy (shown here) takes 2.5 million years to reach Earth, so scientists say the galaxy is 2.5 million light-years away.

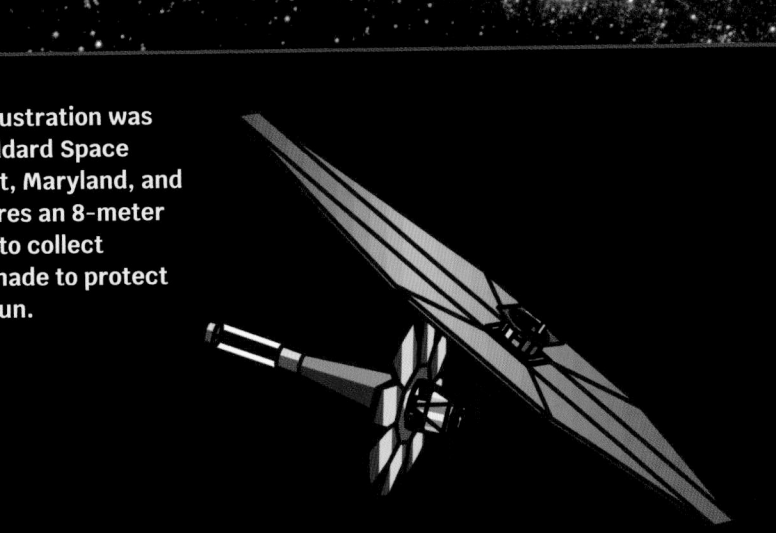

This early NGST design illustration was developed by NASA's Goddard Space Flight Center in Greenbelt, Maryland, and released in 1998. It features an 8-meter (26-foot) primary mirror to collect infrared light and a sunshade to protect the telescope from the Sun.

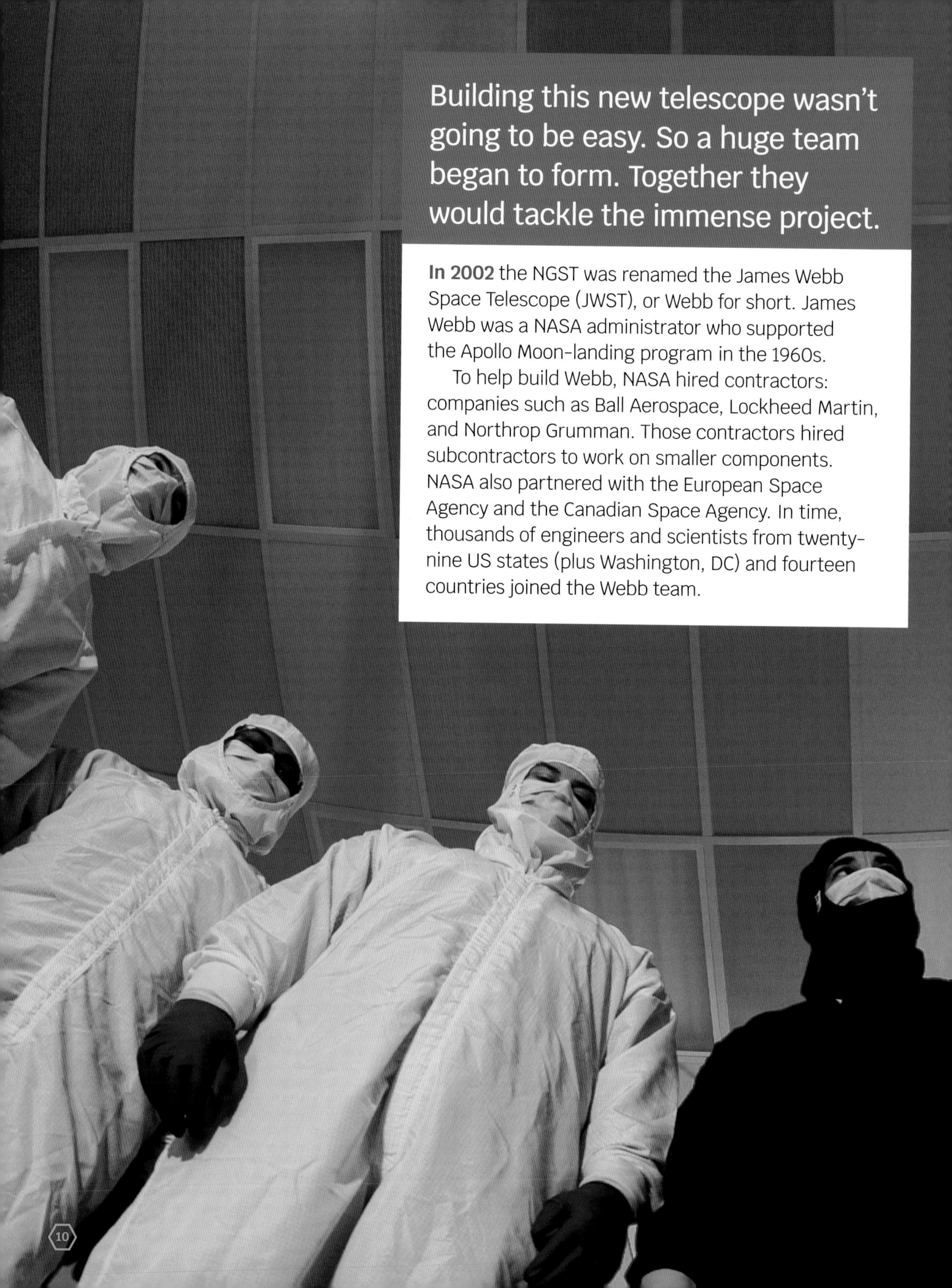

Building this new telescope wasn't going to be easy. So a huge team began to form. Together they would tackle the immense project.

In 2002 the NGST was renamed the James Webb Space Telescope (JWST), or Webb for short. James Webb was a NASA administrator who supported the Apollo Moon-landing program in the 1960s.

To help build Webb, NASA hired contractors: companies such as Ball Aerospace, Lockheed Martin, and Northrop Grumman. Those contractors hired subcontractors to work on smaller components. NASA also partnered with the European Space Agency and the Canadian Space Agency. In time, thousands of engineers and scientists from twenty-nine US states (plus Washington, DC) and fourteen countries joined the Webb team.

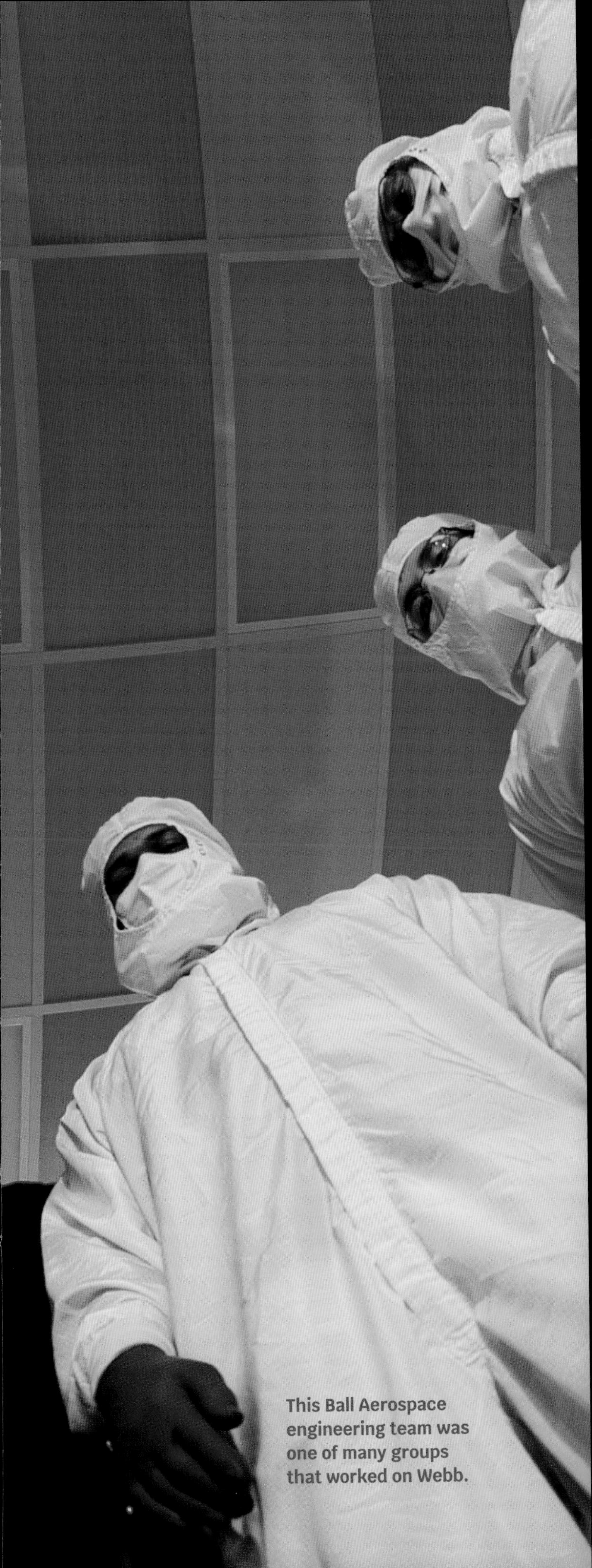

Webb team members at the Goddard Space Flight Center in Greenbelt, Maryland, stand in front of a full-scale model of the James Webb Space Telescope in 2008.

Webb is more than a telescope! It's actually a complex observatory composed of a powerful telescope with many science instruments riding atop a kite-shaped sunshade.

OBSERVING SIDE

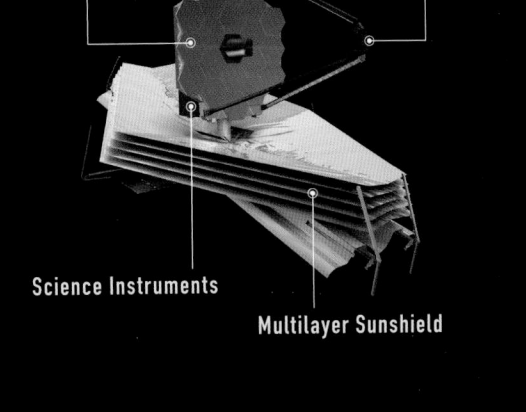

Primary Mirror

Secondary Mirror

Science Instruments

Multilayer Sunshield

SUN-FACING SIDE

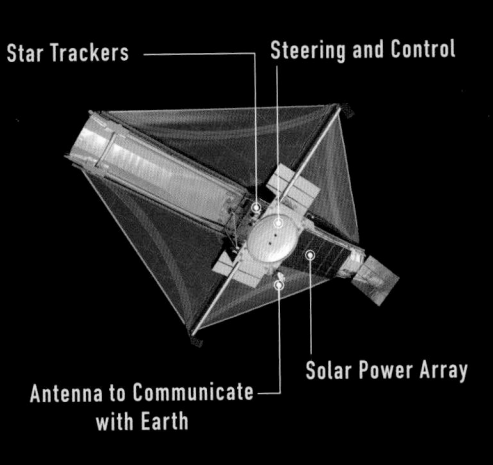

Star Trackers

Steering and Control

Antenna to Communicate with Earth

Solar Power Array

This Ball Aerospace engineering team was one of many groups that worked on Webb.

The team calculated and collaborated. How would Webb's huge mirror fit into a rocket?

One major design challenge was Webb's primary mirror. At 6.6 meters (21.7 feet) across, this colossal mirror was larger than any mirror on any space telescope. In fact, it was way too big to squeeze inside a rocket. So engineers decided to make eighteen smaller hexagonal mirrors and mount them on a structure that could fold up. When the structure was unfolded, the small mirrors would form one giant mirror.

The mirrors also needed to be light enough to be launched by a rocket. So scientists agreed to use a strong, lightweight metal called beryllium. Each beryllium mirror was coated with an ultra-thin layer of gold, an excellent material for reflecting and collecting infrared light.

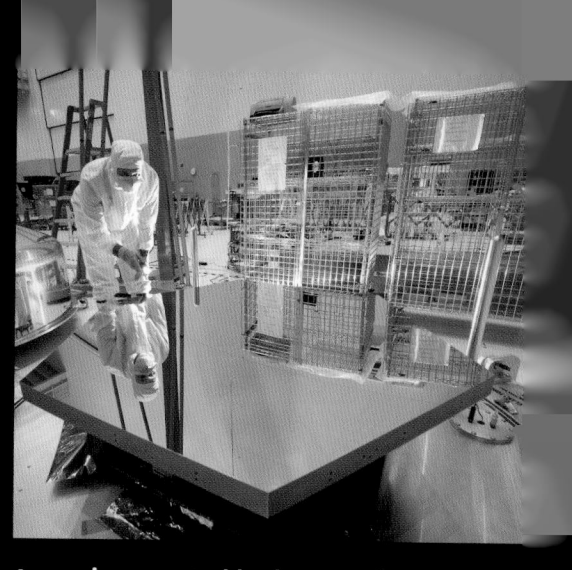

An engineer at Goddard Space Flight Center inspects one of the hexagonal mirrors created by Ball Aerospace in Colorado. Each mirror measures 1.3 meters (4.3 feet) from side to side.

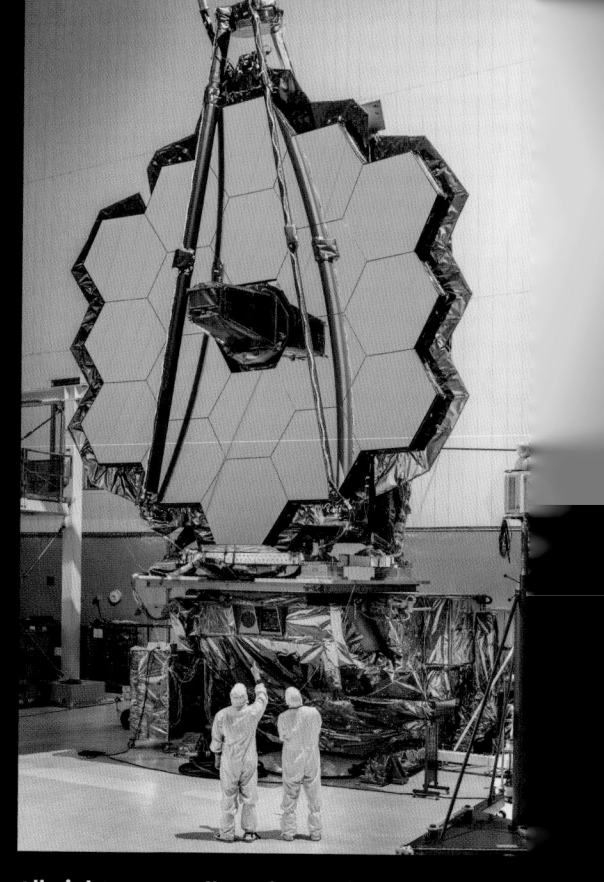

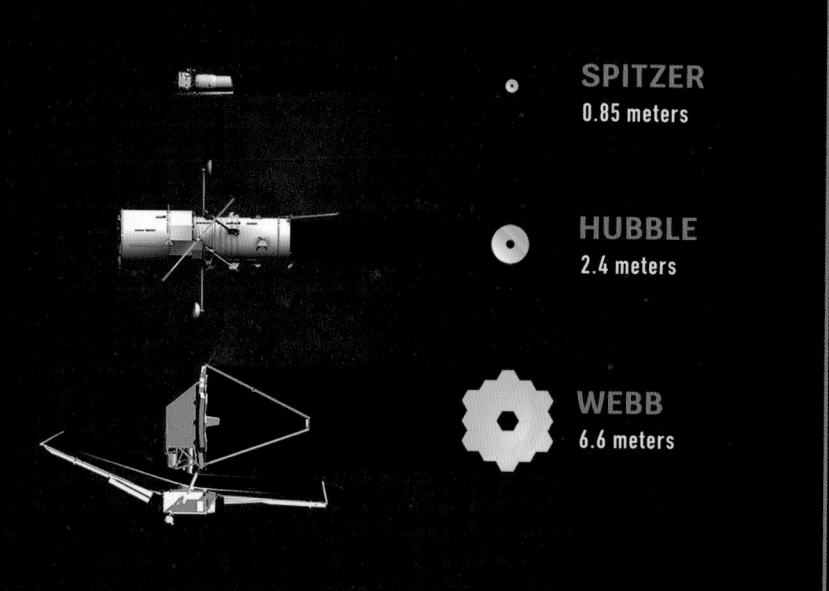

SPITZER
0.85 meters

HUBBLE
2.4 meters

WEBB
6.6 meters

Space telescopes use mirrors to collect light from distant objects. The mirrors reflect the light, focusing it into a narrower beam, and then direct the beam to special instruments in the telescope that analyze the light. Webb's primary mirror is much bigger than Spitzer's or Hubble's primary mirror, which means it can collect a great deal more light.

All eighteen smaller mirrors fit together like puzzle pieces to form the large primary mirror. This mirror is in a special clean room, where everyone must wear a sterile bunny suit over their clothes to protect Webb from contaminants like fabric fibers, hair, and dirt. The room has air filters to capture small particles that could damage Webb's parts.

Webb's primary mirror has two moveable panels, called wings, that have three hexagonal mirrors each. The wings can fold back to create a smaller payload size that fits inside a rocket.

They worried and wondered. Could NASA afford this telescope? Would the telescope get too hot as it orbited the Sun?

Back in 2002 NASA had estimated that Webb would cost $1–3.5 billion. By 2010 the budget had grown to $5.1 billion. People complained, so the US House of Representatives voted to cancel the project. NASA wondered if the dream was over, but space lovers came to the rescue. Scientists, teachers, and students wrote letters pleading with lawmakers to save Webb. And they did! Congress agreed to keep funding the telescope, and the budget was increased to $8 billion. (The total cost for Webb ended up at more than $10 billion.)

One of the scientists' biggest worries was that Webb's delicate instruments might get too hot as the telescope orbited the scorching Sun. So engineers designed a protective sunshield about the size of a tennis court. The sunshield would have five layers, each made of a heat-resistant material called Kapton and coated with shiny aluminum to reflect sunlight.

WEBB'S ORBIT

Once in orbit around the Sun, Webb would be 1.6 million kilometers (1 million miles) from Earth. Its sunshield would always face the Sun to protect the telescope from the Sun's light and heat.

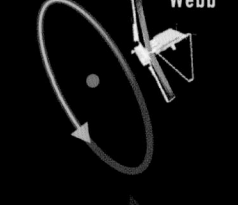

Webb

Webb's Orbit

Earth's Orbit

Earth

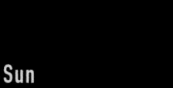

Moon

Sun

Engineers at Northrop Grumman in California conduct tests on a full-sized prototype sunshield. The team practiced deploying the prototype to uncover problems the actual sunshield might encounter in space.

The primary mirror sits atop the actual flight sunshield. The sunshield has space between its layers to dissipate heat and keep the telescope cold.

The Webb team poses proudly after
assembling the ISIM at Goddard Space
Flight Center in 2014. They later attached
the ISIM to the telescope and tested the assembly
to make sure all the components worked together properly.

They assembled and assessed. Would all the parts work together as planned?

Contractors around the world built Webb's various parts, which were then brought together and assembled. In 2014, four light-detecting instruments were joined to create Webb's main payload, the Integrated Science Instrument Module (ISIM). The ISIM was then attached to the telescope.

In 2016 the team began testing the completed telescope. First they did testing to simulate the conditions of a launch. Then they conducted subzero cryogenic testing to see if the telescope could operate in an extremely cold environment with no air.

In 2017 the assembled telescope was moved to Johnson Space Center in Houston to begin cryogenic testing. Engineers suspended the 3,600-kilogram (8,000-pound) telescope from the ceiling to prevent it from experiencing vibrations created by lab pumps, motors, and cars passing by outside.

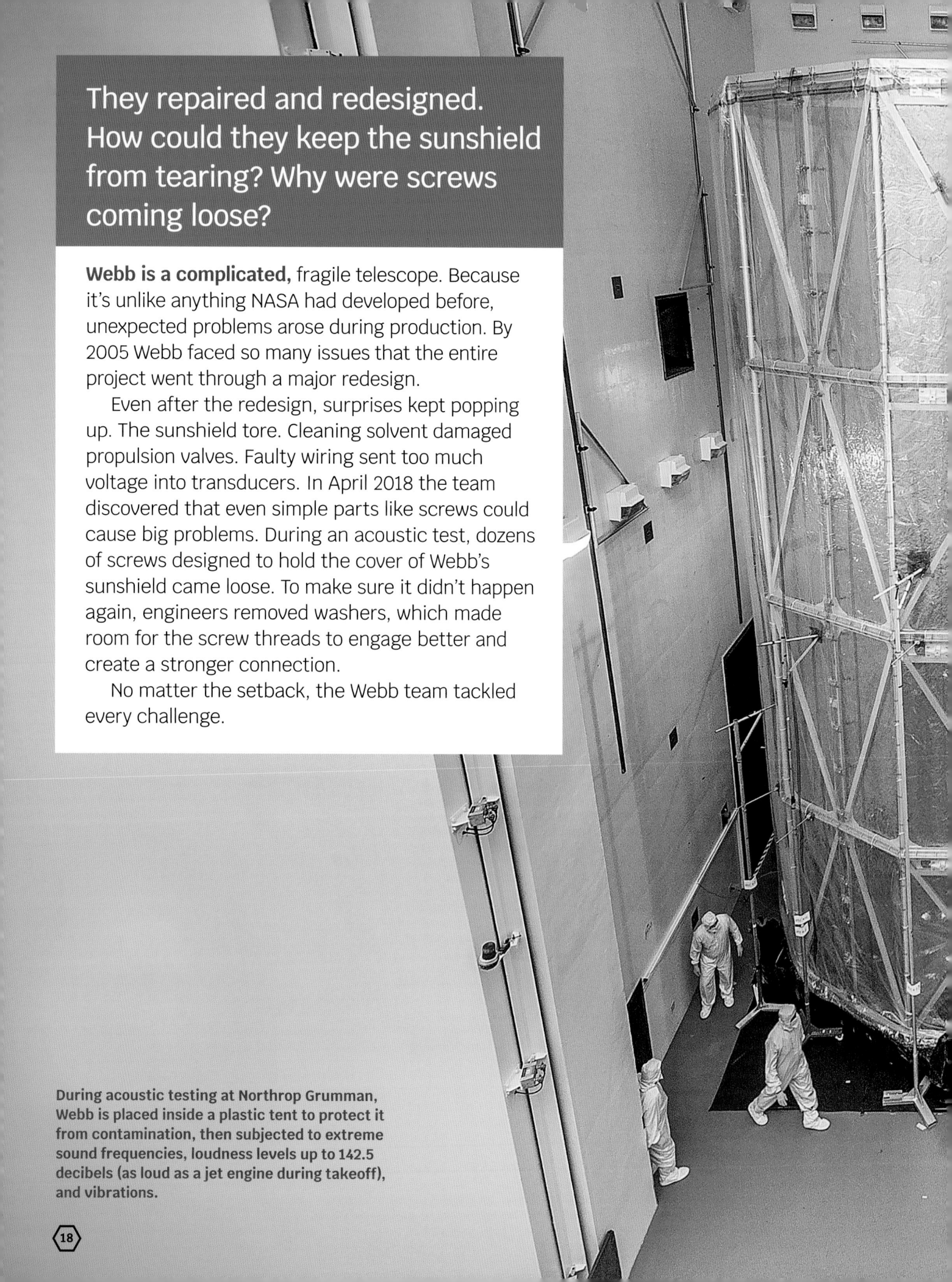

They repaired and redesigned. How could they keep the sunshield from tearing? Why were screws coming loose?

Webb is a complicated, fragile telescope. Because it's unlike anything NASA had developed before, unexpected problems arose during production. By 2005 Webb faced so many issues that the entire project went through a major redesign.

Even after the redesign, surprises kept popping up. The sunshield tore. Cleaning solvent damaged propulsion valves. Faulty wiring sent too much voltage into transducers. In April 2018 the team discovered that even simple parts like screws could cause big problems. During an acoustic test, dozens of screws designed to hold the cover of Webb's sunshield came loose. To make sure it didn't happen again, engineers removed washers, which made room for the screw threads to engage better and create a stronger connection.

No matter the setback, the Webb team tackled every challenge.

During acoustic testing at Northrop Grumman, Webb is placed inside a plastic tent to protect it from contamination, then subjected to extreme sound frequencies, loudness levels up to 142.5 decibels (as loud as a jet engine during takeoff), and vibrations.

Gregory Robinson took over as the JWST program director in March 2018, as Webb faced several budget increases and launch delays. Robinson worked to improve team communication and "schedule efficiency" (how fast tasks were actually completed compared to projected work plans).

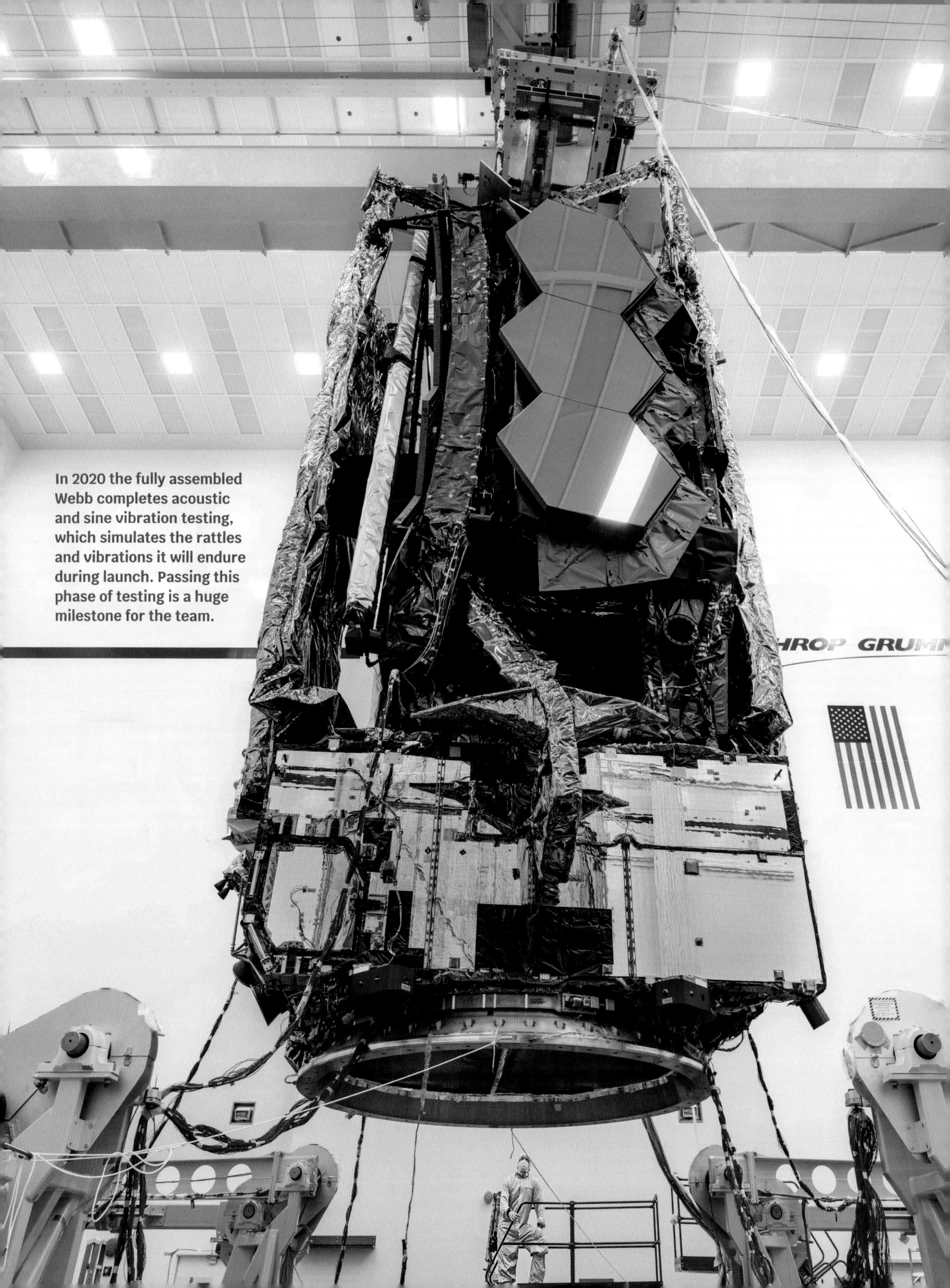

In 2020 the fully assembled Webb completes acoustic and sine vibration testing, which simulates the rattles and vibrations it will endure during launch. Passing this phase of testing is a huge milestone for the team.

They tested and transported. How could they safely move this delicate instrument thousands of miles to its launch site?

In 2019 all of Webb's components were finally assembled at Northrup Grumman. Webb was now a complete observatory. The team was overjoyed. They began more testing to ensure that Webb would survive the jarring vibrations and loud noises of liftoff and the harsh conditions of space. It passed with flying colors!

Then came the next challenge: moving the massive, 6,300-kilogram (14,000-pound) telescope from California to its launch site in South America. Webb was placed inside a custom-made, climate-controlled "suitcase" and loaded onto a cargo transport ship. On September 26, 2021, the ship set off on a 9,300-kilometer (5,800-mile) sea voyage from California to a port in French Guiana. From there, a truck transported the suitcase to Guiana Space Centre in Kourou. To avoid jostling its precious cargo, the truck never went faster than 16 kilometers (10 miles) per hour.

Webb arrives at Port de Pariacabo in French Guiana on October 12, 2021, after its sixteen-day journey by ship from California through the Panama Canal.

Technicians secure the folded-up Webb to the top of the rocket. (The rest of the rocket is below the floor the technicians are walking on.) A tent surrounds Webb to protect it from dust and other contaminants.

They loaded . . .

At the Guiana Space Centre, Webb was slowly hoisted about 40 meters (131 feet) above the ground and placed on top of a mighty Ariane 5 rocket. Technicians bolted it securely in place. A crane then lowered the rocket's nose cone, or protective fairing, over Webb to shield the telescope from heat and pressure during flight.

On December 25, 2021, Webb team members across the globe nervously watched their computer, phone, and television screens. They couldn't believe the dream they'd worked on for so long was about to take flight.

The team uses a laser-guided crane system to lower the fairing over Webb on top of the rocket. Controls inside the fairing provide the proper temperature and humidity level for the telescope.

The Guiana Space Centre team prepares for launch.

The Ariane 5 rocket awaits launch at the Guiana Space Centre.

and launched!

Soon, the countdown began (in French, the language spoken in French Guiana): "Dix. Neuf. Huit. Sept. Six. Cinq. Quatre. Trois. Deux. Unité."

Searing yellow flames engulfed the launchpad as the powerful rocket catapulted Webb toward the heavens.

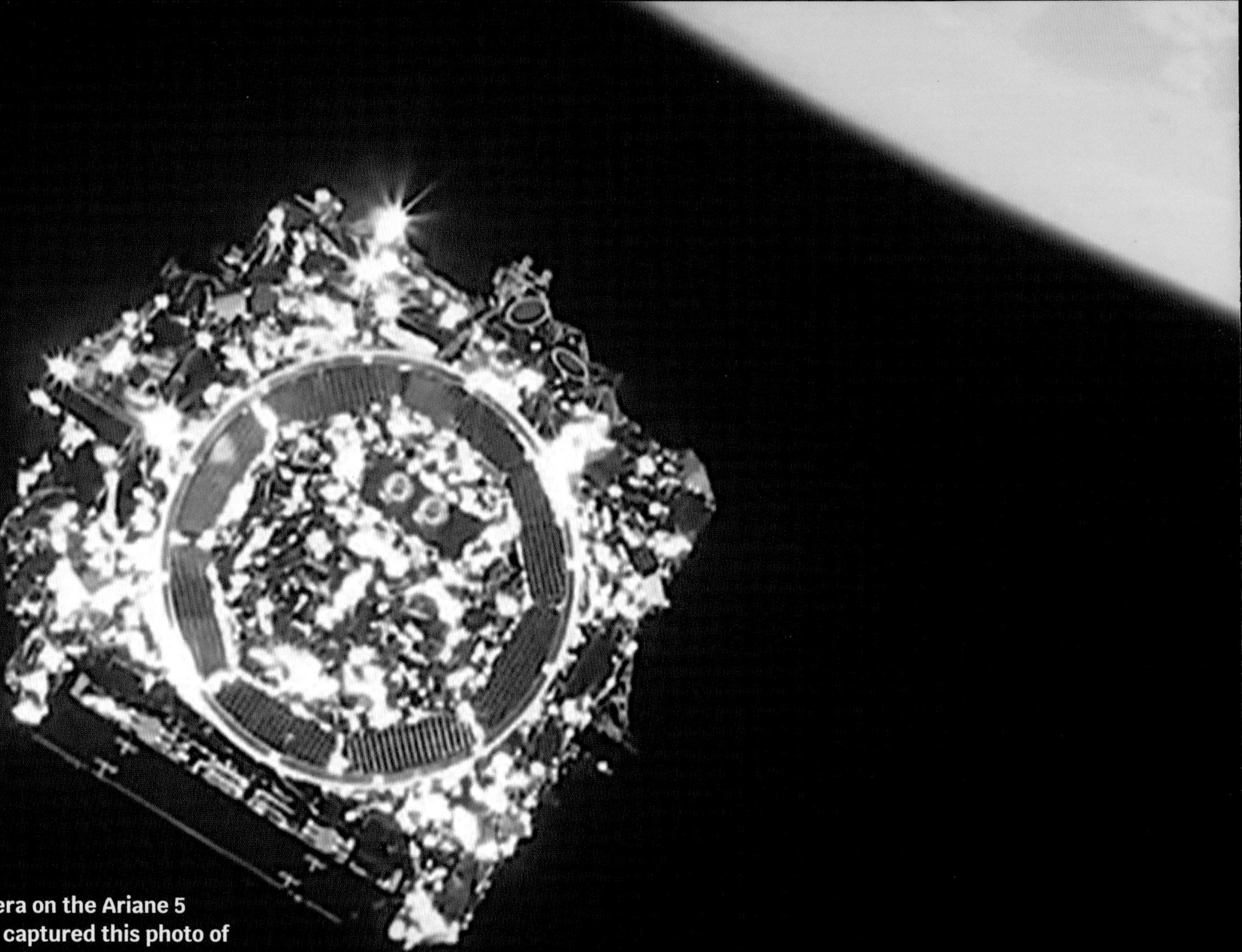

A camera on the Ariane 5 rocket captured this photo of Webb as it soars away from Earth to begin its space mission.

Andria Hagedorn and Matt Wasiak, James Webb Space Telescope timeline coordinators, monitor Webb's second primary mirror wing as it unfolds and moves into position.

Webb departed and deployed.

About thirty minutes after launch, Webb separated from the rocket and began a 1.6-million-kilometer (1-million-mile) journey to its orbiting position around the Sun. During the trek, it slowly unfolded from its stowed configuration.

First it deployed a solar array to make electricity, then an antenna to communicate with Earth. Engineers guided Webb by activating its small rocket engines to make trajectory-correction maneuvers. During the first week in space, technicians remotely deployed the large sunshield.

Soon they began unfolding the primary mirror's wings and latching them in place. The meticulous alignment of the mirror's eighteen segments took about three months. Next the team activated and tested science instruments. Webb practiced tracking moving targets, such as asteroids. Six months after launch, scientists started receiving data from Webb. But the world was still waiting for the telescope's first image.

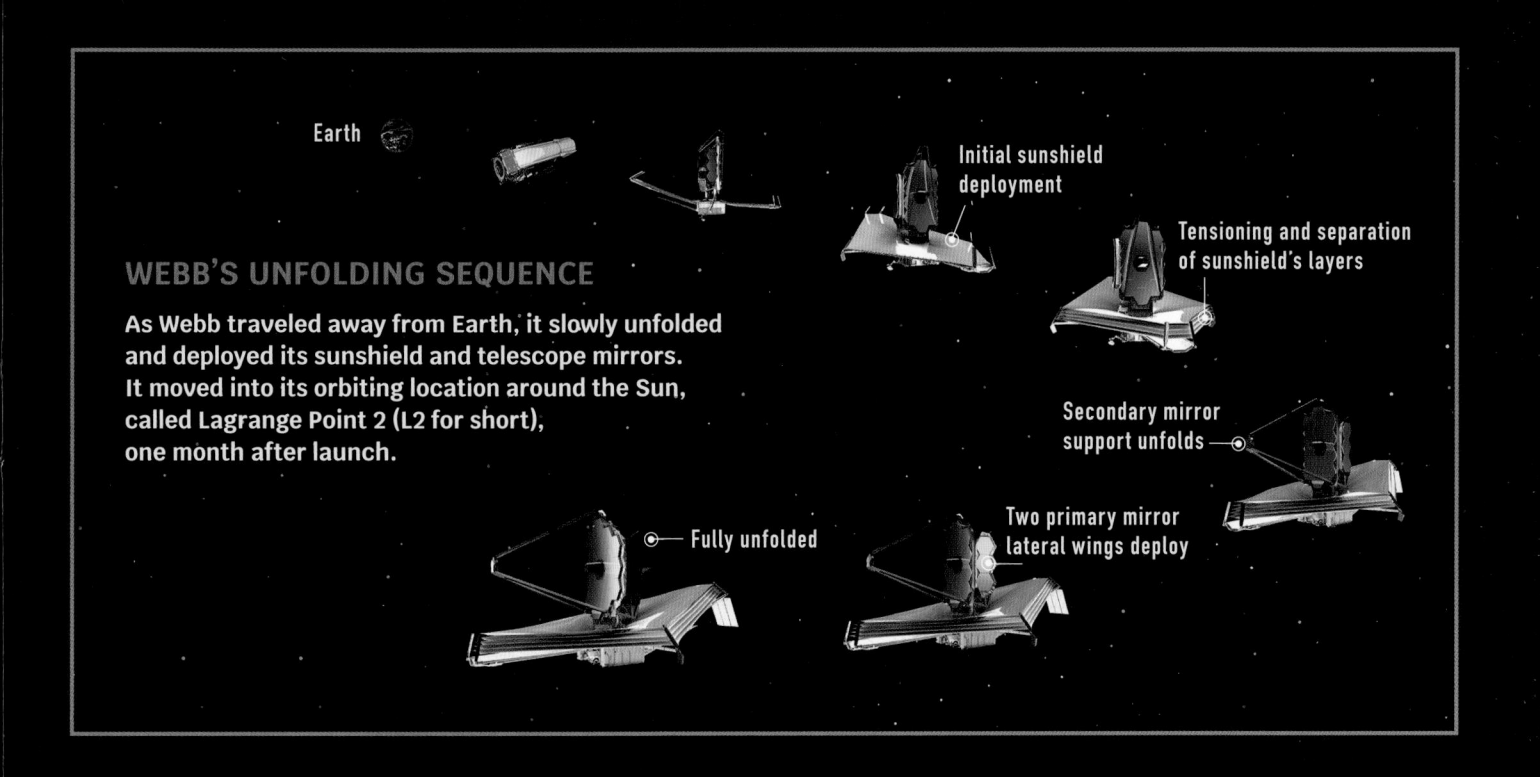

Earth

Initial sunshield deployment

Tensioning and separation of sunshield's layers

WEBB'S UNFOLDING SEQUENCE

As Webb traveled away from Earth, it slowly unfolded and deployed its sunshield and telescope mirrors. It moved into its orbiting location around the Sun, called Lagrange Point 2 (L2 for short), one month after launch.

Secondary mirror support unfolds

Two primary mirror lateral wings deploy

Fully unfolded

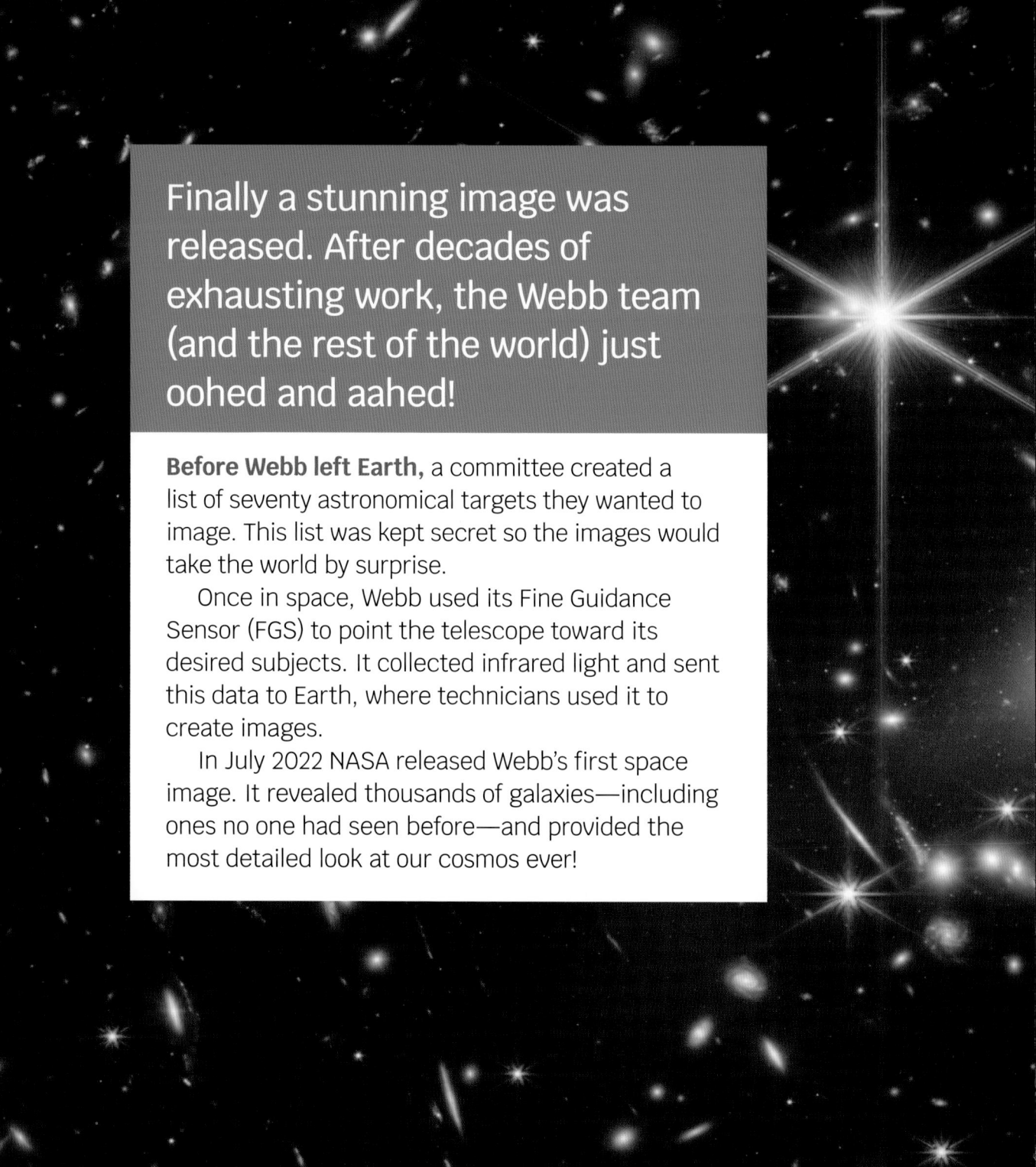

Finally a stunning image was released. After decades of exhausting work, the Webb team (and the rest of the world) just oohed and aahed!

Before Webb left Earth, a committee created a list of seventy astronomical targets they wanted to image. This list was kept secret so the images would take the world by surprise.

Once in space, Webb used its Fine Guidance Sensor (FGS) to point the telescope toward its desired subjects. It collected infrared light and sent this data to Earth, where technicians used it to create images.

In July 2022 NASA released Webb's first space image. It revealed thousands of galaxies—including ones no one had seen before—and provided the most detailed look at our cosmos ever!

Named *Webb's First Deep Field*, Webb's first image reveals galaxy cluster SMACS 0723 as it appeared 4.6 billion years ago. The remarkable clarity of the image astounded people around the globe.

This breathtaking image demonstrates how Webb peers through cosmic dust to investigate star formation. The part that looks like mountains and valleys is the edge of a stellar nursery in the Carina Nebula. Stellar nurseries are places where new stars are born.

Webb's Wonderful
Discoveries

It took twenty thousand people thirty years to build and deploy the James Webb Space Telescope. Due to their ingenuity and teamwork, we can explore the vast cosmos from the comfort of our own tiny planet. Every minute of every day (even now as you read this book), Webb is soaring through space, expanding our understanding of the universe.

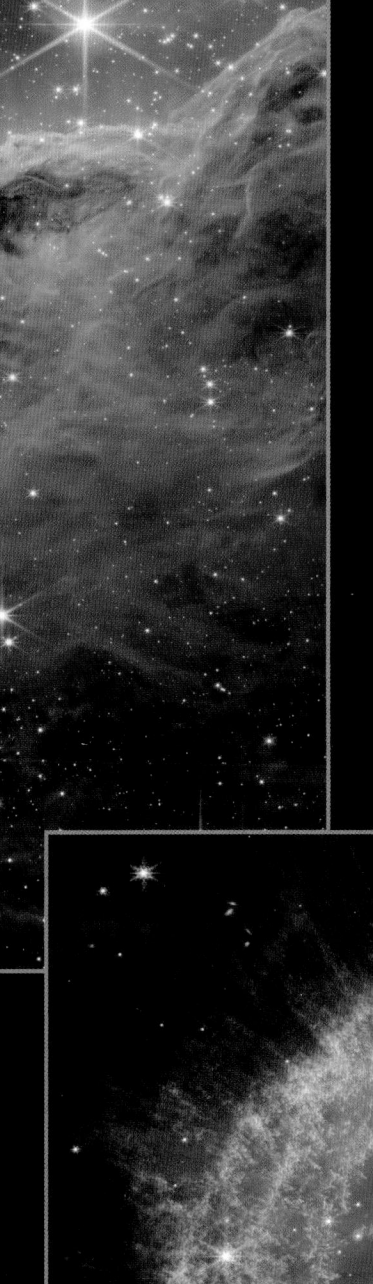

Webb's clear image of the Cartwheel Galaxy helped scientists discover details about its central black hole and outer ring. The image includes two other galaxies on the left.

This Webb image shows the Ring Nebula, created by a dying star throwing off its outer layers. Scientists were surprised to find molecules called polycyclic aromatic hydrocarbons (PAHs) within the nebula's inner ring and strange spikes radiating from its outer ring.

Although Wolf-Rayet stars are some of the brightest and most massive stars known to scientists, they are rarely observed. Only some massive stars go through a Wolf-Rayet phase, and that phase is very brief. This Webb image captures the star Wolf-Rayet 124 and its halo of gas and dust.

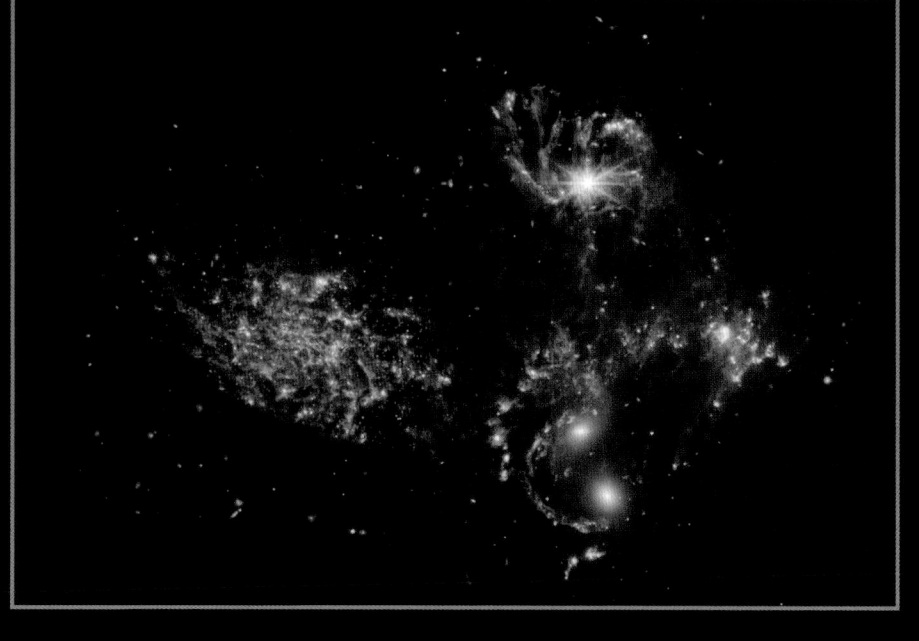

Webb's powerful Mid-Infrared Instrument (MIRI) reveals new details of Stephan's Quintet, a group of five galaxies. This image provides insights into how galactic interactions may have driven galaxy evolution long ago. The galaxy at the top, named NGC 7319, contains a massive black hole 24 million times the mass of the Sun.

Webb's image of Jupiter shows incredible details, such as the planet's huge, ongoing storm, the Great Red Spot (which appears white in the image). Jupiter's north and south poles are in the greenish-yellow areas.

In this close-up image, sunlike stars are born in a star-forming region called Rho Ophiuchi. Jets of gas shoot from the young stars and light up the area.

Author's Note

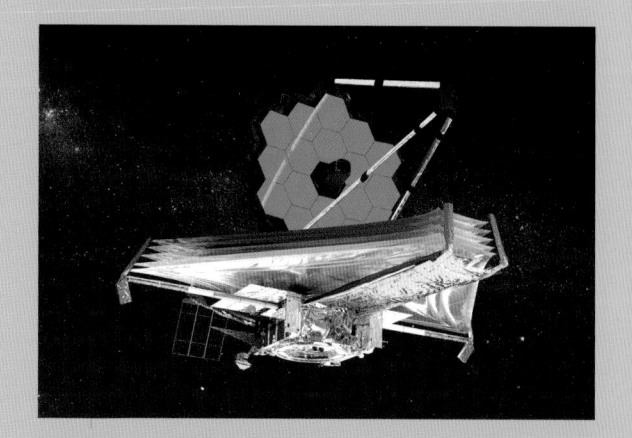

As an engineer who has worked on rockets, I'm extremely curious about space. It seems the more I learn about our limitless universe, the more I want to know. When I first heard about the James Webb Space Telescope project decades ago, I was blown away by its lofty goals. And to be honest, I wondered if such an ambitious project could become a reality. But—thanks to visionaries, problem solvers, and science fans who never stopped believing in Webb— it did.

As the days counted down to the release of the first Webb image in 2022, I could hardly contain my excitement. What would the most powerful telescope ever launched into space discover? The answer, as we've seen with our own eyes, is a lot! Webb looked back in time at a sparkling galaxy cluster more than 5 billion light-years away. It gave us a peek at what ancient galaxies looked like 13 billion years ago. It's even observing the birth and death of stars and studying exoplanets to see if any could support life. Today the James Webb Space Telescope faithfully continues its mission as it makes more discoveries beyond our wildest dreams!

President Joseph Biden unveils the first full-color Webb image at a White House event on July 11, 2022. On-screen (from top) are Thomas Zurbuchen, Associate Administrator for NASA's Science Mission Directorate; Nancy Levenson, Deputy Director of the Space Telescope Science Institute (STScI); and Gregory Robinson, James Webb Space Telescope Program Director.

Artist's conception of the James Webb Space Telescope orbiting the Sun.

Webb's Light-Detecting Instruments

Webb's primary mirror collects light and reflects it onto a smaller secondary mirror, which then sends the light to four instruments located in the Integrated Science Instrument Module (ISIM).

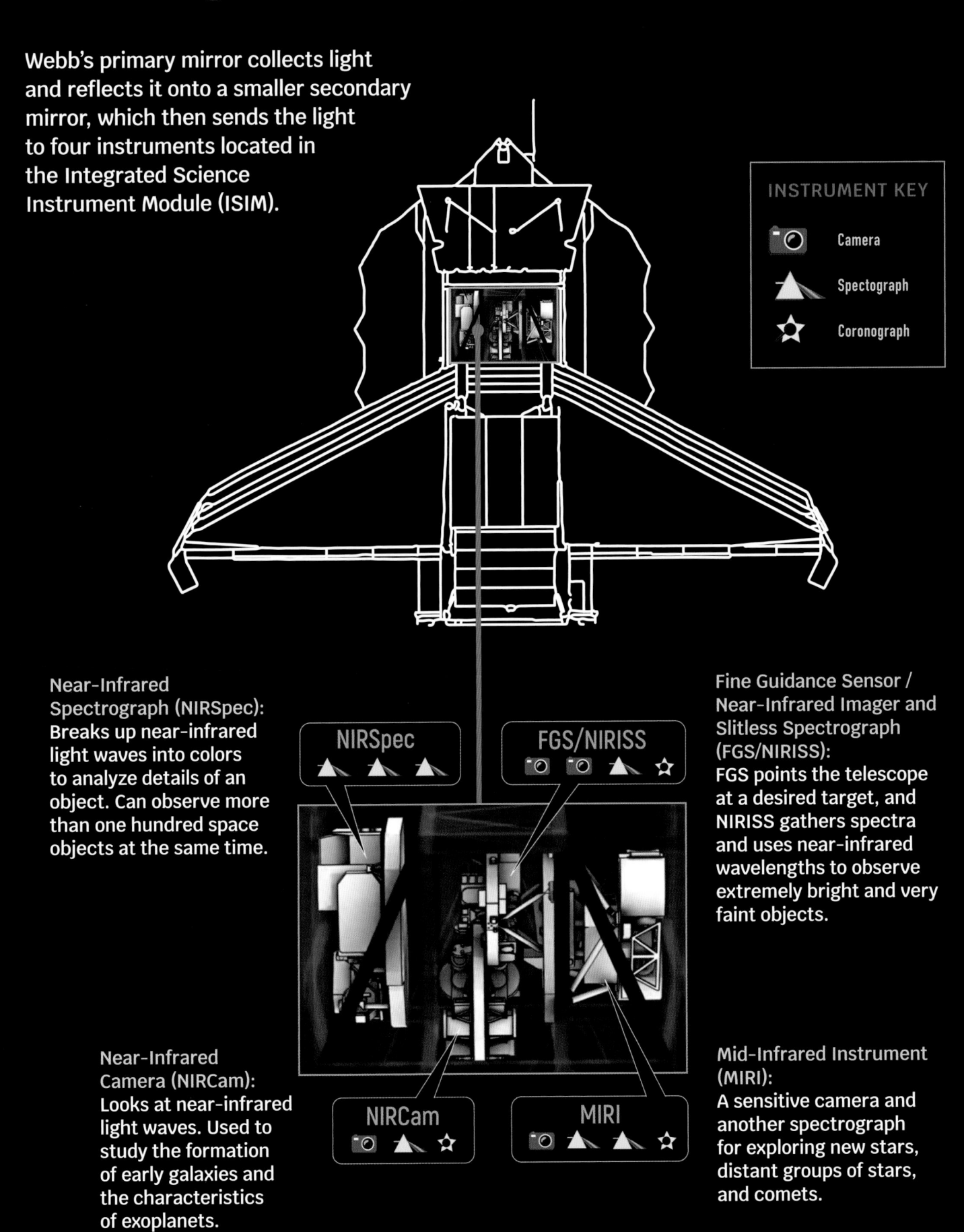

INSTRUMENT KEY

Camera

Spectrograph

Coronograph

Near-Infrared Spectrograph (NIRSpec): Breaks up near-infrared light waves into colors to analyze details of an object. Can observe more than one hundred space objects at the same time.

NIRSpec

FGS/NIRISS

Fine Guidance Sensor / Near-Infrared Imager and Slitless Spectrograph (FGS/NIRISS): FGS points the telescope at a desired target, and NIRISS gathers spectra and uses near-infrared wavelengths to observe extremely bright and very faint objects.

Near-Infrared Camera (NIRCam): Looks at near-infrared light waves. Used to study the formation of early galaxies and the characteristics of exoplanets.

NIRCam

MIRI

Mid-Infrared Instrument (MIRI): A sensitive camera and another spectrograph for exploring new stars, distant groups of stars, and comets.

NASA's Great Observatories

NASA's Great Observatories program enables astronomers to compare multiple images of the same space object, created using different wavelengths of light. These comparisons have led to remarkable discoveries.

Before deploying Webb, NASA studied the cosmos with four great space observatories. Today, Webb's clear, detailed images are answering even more questions about the wonders of space.

This image of the Antennae Galaxies is a composite created by data from the Chandra X-ray Observatory (blue), the Hubble Space Telescope (gold and brown), and the Spitzer Space Telescope (red). The long antenna-like arms were produced by a collision of two galaxies, which began more than 100 million years ago and is still going on today.

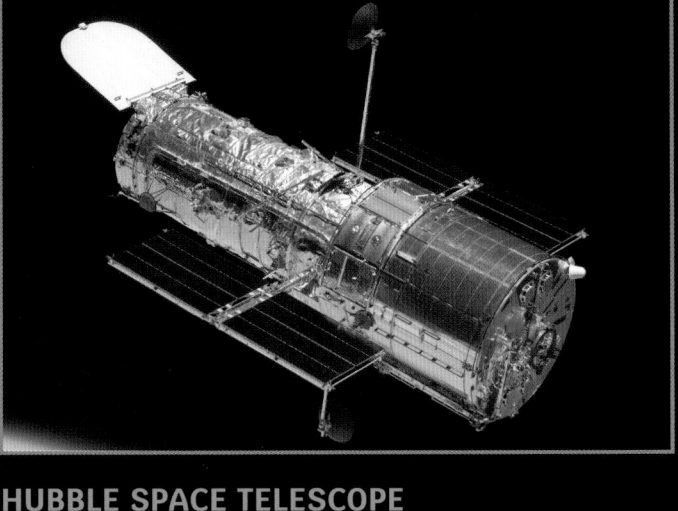

HUBBLE SPACE TELESCOPE (1990–PRESENT)

As it orbits 610 kilometers (380 miles) above Earth, Hubble observes in near-infrared, ultraviolet, and visible wavelengths. It has generated thousands of images and provided astronomers with new details about the history of stars and galaxies, and proof that black holes exist.

COMPTON GAMMA RAY OBSERVATORY (1991–2000)

Weighing more than 15,000 kilograms (17 tons), Compton was the heaviest payload ever flown when space shuttle Atlantis carried it into space. Compton made discoveries about violent, high-energy processes such as gamma-ray quasars, rare gamma-ray pulsars, and gamma-ray bursts (huge space explosions).

CHANDRA X-RAY OBSERVATORY (1999–PRESENT)

With its extremely smooth mirrors, Chandra creates images twenty-five times sharper than those from any previous X-ray telescope. Astronomers have used its images to study black holes, supernovas, dark matter, and more.

SPITZER SPACE TELESCOPE (2003–2020)

Spitzer detected infrared energy, which can penetrate clouds of gas and dust in space. Using Spitzer, astronomers peered through dense clouds to see stellar nurseries, the centers of galaxies, and newly forming planetary systems.

Webb's detailed view of Uranus shows the planet's north polar cap, its inner and outer rings, and nine of its twenty-seven moons.

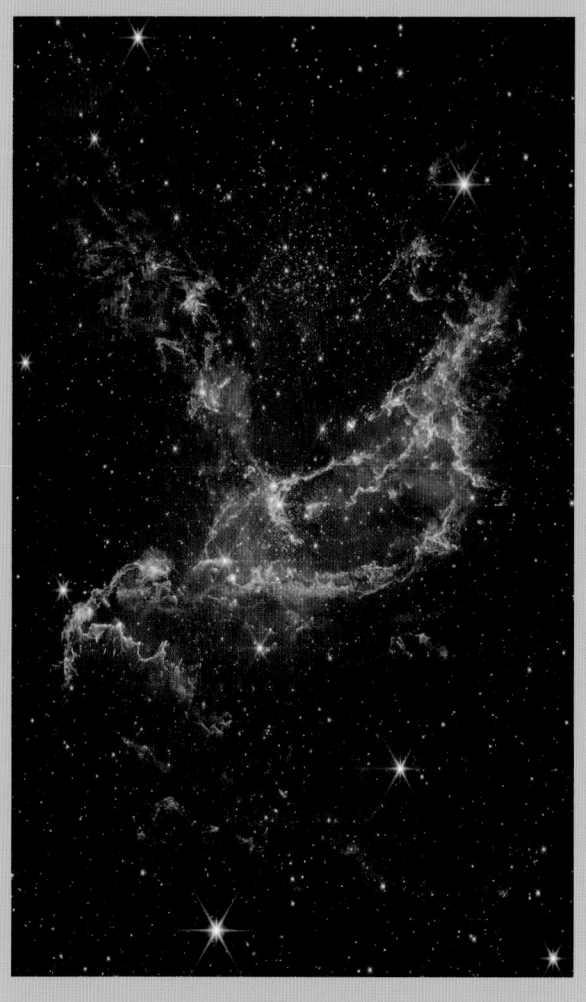

Webb's image of NGC 346, a star-forming region, reveals the smallest baby stars (protostars) ever seen. Webb's sensitive instruments also allow scientists to study the dust in the disks of gas around these protostars for the first time.

Acknowledgments

Sincere thanks to Dr. Jonathan P. Gardner, Deputy Senior Project Scientist, James Webb Space Telescope, NASA's Goddard Space Flight Center; Sandra M. Irish, Mechanical Systems Lead Structures Engineer, James Webb Space Telescope, NASA's Goddard Space Flight Center; and Talia Sepersky, planetarium educator at the Museum of Science, Boston, for their help with this book.

Resources for Kids

Print out this free pdf and build a 1:48 scale model of Webb:
https://webb.nasa.gov/resources/JWST_model_1-48scale_final-parts.pdf

Watch a video of Webb's launch:
https://www.youtube.com/watch?v=9tXlqWldVVk&ab_channel=JamesWebbSpaceTelescope%28JWST%29

See how Webb unfolded in space in this animation:
https://www.youtube.com/watch?v=RzGLKQ7_KZQ&ab_channel=JamesWebbSpaceTelescope%28JWST%29

Learn more about how Webb works in this video:
https://www.youtube.com/watch?v=4P8fKd0IVOs&ab_channel=SmarterEveryDay

Webb's sharp image of Saturn shows the planet's bright, icy rings and three of its moons, Dione, Enceladus, and Tethys.

Selected Bibliography

Chang, Kenneth. "He Fixed NASA's Giant Space Telescope, Reluctantly." *New York Times*, July 11, 2022. https://www.nytimes.com/2022/07/11/science/greg-robinson-webb-telescope-nasa.html.

NASA. "The International Webb Team." https://science.nasa.gov/mission/webb/webb-team.

NASA. "NASA's James Webb Space Telescope." https://www.flickr.com/photos/nasawebbtelescope/.

NASA. "Webb Observatory." https://science.nasa.gov/mission/webb/spacecraftoverview.

NASA Goddard Space Flight Center. "James Webb Space Telescope." https://jwst.nasa.gov/.

Space Telescope Science Institute. "Webb Space Telescope." https://webbtelescope.org/.

A brown dwarf grows like a star, becoming denser and denser, but never gets dense enough or hot enough to turn into a star. Webb found this tiny brown dwarf, the smallest free-floating one to date!

This exciting image shows two actively forming stars named Herbig-Haro 46/47 in the bright orange-white section in the middle. Gas and dust are feeding their growth, but it's a slow process. It will take millions of years for these baby stars to grow into full-fledged stars.

Text copyright © 2024 by Suzanne Slade
All images in the public domain or used with permission.

All rights reserved, including the right of reproduction in whole or in part in any form. Charlesbridge and colophon are registered trademarks of Charlesbridge Publishing, Inc.

At the time of publication, all URLs printed in this book were accurate and active. Charlesbridge and the author are not responsible for the content or accessibility of any website.

Published by Charlesbridge
9 Galen Street, Watertown, MA 02472
(617) 926-0329
www.charlesbridge.com

Library of Congress Cataloging-in-Publication Data
Names: Slade, Suzanne, author.
Title: Unlocking the Universe: the cosmic discoveries of the Webb Space Telescope / Suzanne Slade.
Description: Watertown, MA: Charlesbridge, [2024] | Includes bibliographical references. | Audience: Ages 6–9 | Audience: Grades K–1 | Summary: "A massive team of dedicated scientists designed, built, and deployed the James Webb Space Telescope. Now the world's most powerful telescope is in space, expanding our understanding of the universe. Illustrated with NASA photos and reviewed for accuracy by members of the Webb team."—Provided by publisher.
Identifiers: LCCN 2023030505 (print) | LCCN 2023030506 (ebook) | ISBN 9781623544591 (hardcover) | ISBN 9781632894083 (ebook)
Subjects: LCSH: James Webb Space Telescope (Spacecraft)—Juvenile literature. | Space telescopes—Juvenile literature. | Astronomy—Observations—Juvenile literature.
Classification: LCC QB500.269.S53 2023 (print) | LCC QB500.269 (ebook) | DDC 522/.2919—dc23/eng/20231025
LC record available at https://lccn.loc.gov/2023030505
LC ebook record available at https://lccn.loc.gov/2023030506

Printed in China
(hc) 10 9 8 7 6 5 4 3 2 1

Display type set in BroadbandICG, © Image Club Graphics, Inc.
Text type set in Krub, © The Krub Project Authors
Printed by 1010 Printing International Limited in Huizhou, Guangdong, China
Production supervision by Nicole Turner
Designed by Cathleen Schaad

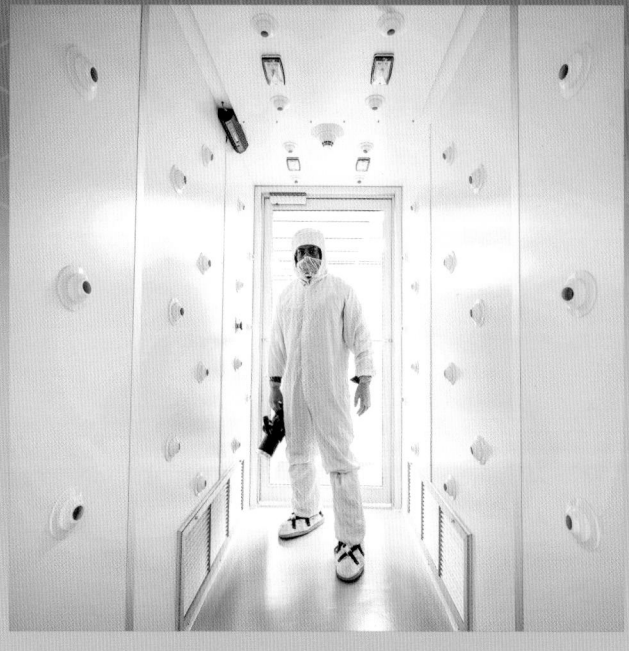

Photographer Chris Gunn took this self-portrait before entering a clean room to photograph Webb. He wore a bunny suit and cleaned his camera gear to avoid bringing contaminants into the room. Gunn took many of the photos featured in this book.

IMAGE CREDITS
All Webb Space Telescope images by NASA, ESA, CSA.

Front cover, p. 1 and **p. 3** (in circle): Illustration of Webb Space Telescope: NASA/dima_zel. Cropped image used under a Creative Commons 4.0 license. Original image available online at https://noirlab.edu/public/images/webb_telescope-orig/. **pp. 4–5**: NASA, ESA, and the Hubble Heritage Team (STScI/AURA). **p. 4** (bottom): NASA/JPL-Caltech. **p. 5** (top): NASA and J. Olmstead (STScI).* **pp. 6–7**: NASA/JPL-Caltech/STScI. **p. 7** (bottom): NASA, ESA, CXC, JPL, Caltech, and STScI. **pp. 8–9**: NASA/JPL-Caltech. **p. 9** (bottom): NASA. **pp. 10–11**: NASA/Drew Noel.* **p. 11** (top): NASA/GSFC; (bottom): NASA, ESA, CSA, Joyce Kang (STScI). **p. 12** (left): STScI (image); NASA, ESA, STScI (3D model); (top right): NASA/Chris Gunn;* (bottom right): NASA/Goddard/Chris Gunn. **pp. 13** and **14–15** (top): NASA/Chris Gunn.* **p. 14** (bottom): NASA, ESA, CSA, STScI. **pp. 15** (bottom), **16–17, 17** (bottom right), **18–19**: NASA/Chris Gunn.* **p. 19** (top right): NASA. **pp. 20, 21,** and **22** (top left): NASA/Chris Gunn.* **p. 22** (bottom left): ESA/CNES/Arianespace. **p. 22** (bottom right), **23, 24, 25** (left and right): NASA/Bill Ingalls.* **pp. 26–27**: ESA, NASA. **p. 26** (bottom): NASA/Bill Ingalls.* **p. 27** (bottom): NASA, ESA, CSA, Joyce Kang (STScI). **p. 34** (top): NASA/Bill Ingalls;* (bottom): NASA GSFC/CIL/Adriana Manrique Gutierrez.* **p. 35**: NASA, ESA, CSA, STScI. **p. 36**: NASA/CXC/SAO/JPL-Caltech/STScI. **p. 37** (top left): NASA; (top right): NASA/Ken Cameron; (bottom left): MSFC; (bottom right): NASA/JPL-Caltech. **p. 40**: Chris Gunn.*

* Cropped, rotated, and/or redesigned image used under a Creative Commons 2.0 license. Original image available online at https://www.flickr.com/photos/nasawebbtelescope/albums.

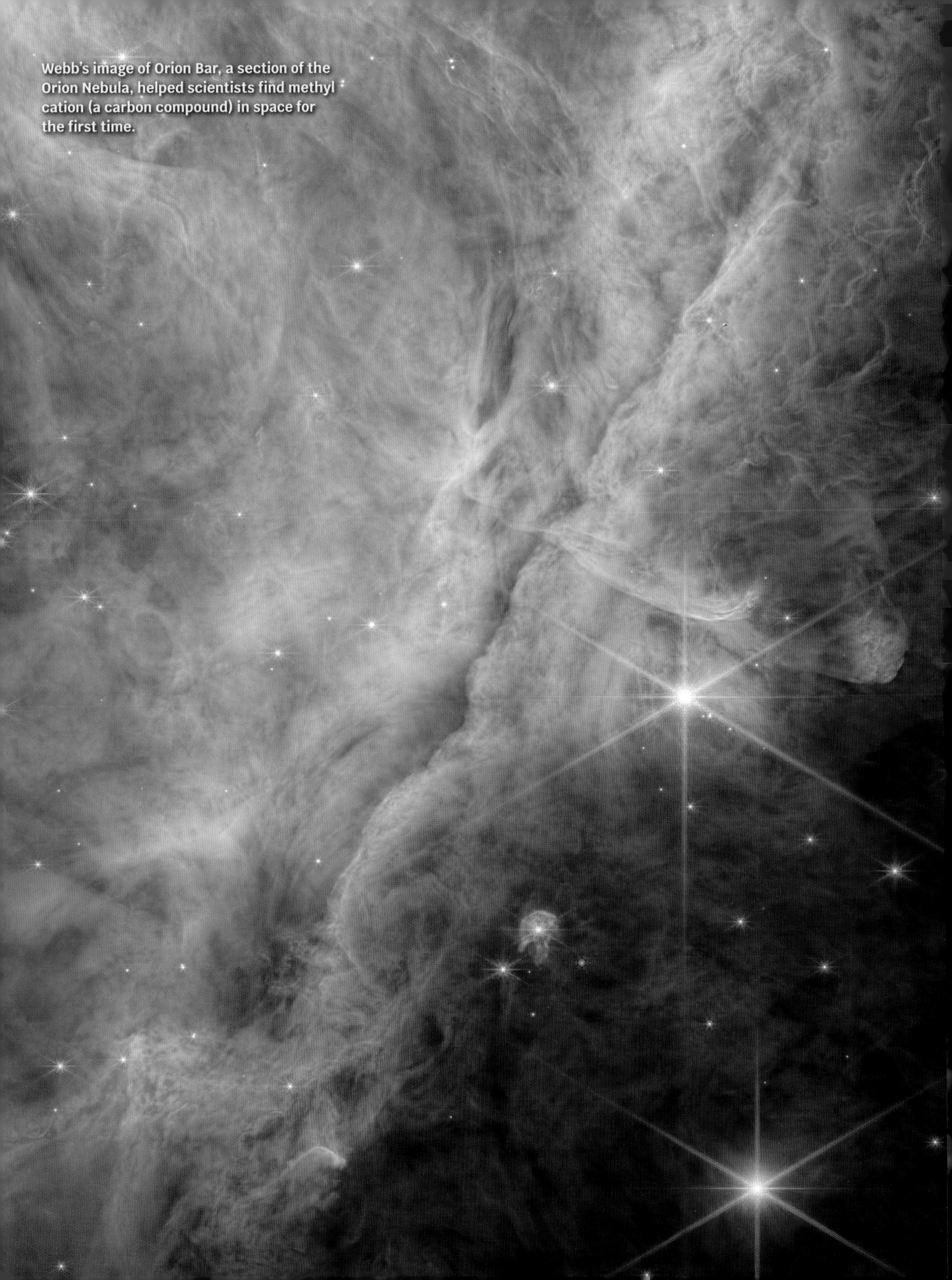

Webb's image of Orion Bar, a section of the Orion Nebula, helped scientists find methyl cation (a carbon compound) in space for the first time.

This Webb image of the Tarantula Nebula reveals thousands of young stars that were previously hidden by cosmic dust.